A
Short
History
of the
Blockade

LEANNE BETASAMOSAKE SIMPSON

A
Short
History
of the
Blockade

Giant Beavers,
Diplomacy, and
Regeneration in
Nishnaabewin

CLC KREISEL LECTURE SERIES

Canadian Literature Centre
Centre de littérature canadienne

UNIVERSITY *of* **ALBERTA** PRESS

Published by

University of Alberta Press
1–16 Rutherford Library South
11204 89 Avenue NW
Edmonton, Alberta, Canada T6G 2J4
uap.ualberta.ca

and

Canadian Literature Centre /
Centre de littérature canadienne
3–5 Humanities Centre
University of Alberta
Edmonton, Alberta, Canada T6G 2E5
www.abclc.ca

LIBRARY AND ARCHIVES CANADA
CATALOGUING IN PUBLICATION

Title: A short history of the blockade : giant
    beavers, diplomacy, and regeneration in
    Nishnaabewin / Leanne Betasamosake
    Simpson.
Names: Simpson, Leanne Betasamosake,
    1971– author. | Canadian Literature Centre,
    publisher.
Series: Henry Kreisel lecture series.
Description: Series statement: CLC Kreisel
    lecture series
Identifiers: Canadiana (print) 20200374109 |
    Canadiana (ebook) 20200386360 |
    ISBN 9781772125382 (softcover) |
    ISBN 9781772125504 (EPUB) |
    ISBN 9781772125528 (PDF)
Subjects: LCSH: Ojibwa literature—Canada—
    History and criticism. | LCSH: Beavers. |
    LCSH: Dams. | LCSH: Social justice—
    Canada. | LCSH: Protest movements—
    Canada. | LCSH: Indigenous peoples—
    Canada—Government relations. | LCSH:
    Indigenous peoples—Canada—Social
    conditions. | LCSH: Indigenous peoples—
    Canada—Social life and customs. | LCSH:
    Storytelling.
Classification: LCC PM853.5 .S56 2021 |
    DDC C897/.33309581—dc23

First edition, second printing, 2021.
First printed and bound in Canada by
Houghton Boston Printers, Saskatoon,
Saskatchewan.
Copyediting and proofreading by
Joanne Muzak.

The Canadian Literature Centre acknowledges
the support of Dr. Eric Schloss and the Faculty
of Arts for the CLC Kreisel Lecture delivered by
Leanne Betasamosake Simpson in March 2020
at the University of Alberta.

University of Alberta Press gratefully
acknowledges the support received for its
publishing program from the Government
of Canada, the Canada Council for the Arts,
and the Government of Alberta through the
Alberta Media Fund.

To my relatives the Amikwag and all of the land defenders,
water defenders, body, mind and spirit defenders,
life protectors, and anti-colonial world builders.

FOREWORD
The CLC *Kreisel Lecture Series*

The CLC Kreisel Lectures bring together writers, readers, students, scholars, teachers—and with this book, publisher and research centre—in an open, inclusive, and critical literary forum. The Series has also fostered a beautiful partnership between the CLC and CBC Radio's *Ideas*, which has produced exciting broadcasts that feature the lecturers themselves—including this one by Leanne Betasamosake Simpson, and ones by Michael Crummey, Heather O'Neill, Margaret Atwood, and Lynn Coady—and further probe each lecture's topic. Through this partnership, the Kreisel Lectures are able to reach an audience of over a million listeners. The series raises a myriad of issues, at times painful, at times joyful, but always salient and far-reaching: Indigenous resurgence, oppression and social justice, cultural identity, place and displacement, the spoils of history, storytelling, censorship, language, reading in a digital age, literary history, and personal memory. The Series confronts subjects that concern us all within the specificities of our contemporary experience, whatever our differences. In the spirit of free and honest dialogue, it does so with thoughtfulness and depth as well as humour and grace.

These public lectures also set out to honour Professor Henry Kreisel's legacy in an annual public forum. Author, University Professor, and Officer of the Order of Canada, Henry Kreisel was born in Vienna into a Jewish family in 1922. He left his homeland for England in 1938 and was interned, in Canada, for eighteen months during the Second World War. After studying at the University of Toronto, he began teaching in 1947 at the University of Alberta, and served as Chair of English from 1961 until 1970. He served as Vice-President (Academic) from 1970 to 1975, and was named University Professor in 1975, the highest scholarly award bestowed on its faculty members by the University of Alberta. Professor Kreisel was an inspiring and beloved teacher who taught generations of students to love literature and was among the first to bring the experience of the immigrant to modern Canadian literature. He died in Edmonton in 1991. His works include two novels, *The Rich Man* (1948) and *The Betrayal* (1964), and a collection of short stories, *The Almost Meeting* (1981). His internment diary, alongside critical essays on his writing, appears in *Another Country: Writings by and about Henry Kreisel* (1985).

The generosity of Professor Kreisel's teaching at the University of Alberta profoundly inspires the CLC in its public outreach, research pursuits, and continued commitment to the ever-growing richness, complexity, and diversity of writings in Canada. The Centre embraces Henry Kreisel's pioneering focus on the knowledge of one's own literatures. It is in his memory that we seek to foster better understanding of our difficult world, which literature can help us reimagine and even transform.

The Canadian Literature Centre was established in 2006, thanks to the leadership gift of the noted Edmontonian bibliophile, Dr. Eric Schloss.

MARIE CARRIÈRE
Director, Canadian Literature Centre
Edmonton, June 2020

LIMINAIRE

La Collection des Conférences Kreisel du CLC

Les Conférences Kreisel du CLC rassemblent écrivains et
écrivaines, lecteurs et lectrices, étudiants et étudiantes,
chercheurs et chercheuses, enseignants et enseignantes—et
grâce à ce livre, éditeur et centre de recherche—dans un
forum littéraire ouvert, inclusif et critique. La collection
entretient aussi un magnifique partenariat entre le CLC et
Ideas de CBC Radio dont les radiodiffusions mettent en
vedette les conférenciers et conférencières—y compris
Leanne Betasamosake Simpson ainsi que Michael Crummey,
Heather O'Neill, Margaret Atwood et Lynn Coady—
interrogeant de plus près les thèmes de leur conférence pour
un public de plus d'un million. La collection met en valeur de
nombreuses problématiques, parfois douloureuses, parfois
joyeuses, or toujours saillantes et considérables: résurgence
autochtone, oppression et justice sociale, identité culturelle,
lieu et déplacement, dépouilles de l'histoire, narration,
censure, langage, lecture à l'ère numérique, histoire

littéraire et mémoire personnelle. La collection s'affronte aux questions qui nous concernent tous et toutes selon les spécificités de notre vécu contemporain, peu importent nos différences. Dans une intention de dialogue libre et honnête, elle se produit dans l'ardeur et la profondeur intellectuelles ainsi que l'humour et l'élégance.

Ces conférences publiques et annuelles se consacrent à perpétuer la mémoire du Professeur Henry Kreisel. Auteur, professeur universitaire et Officier de l'Ordre du Canada, Henry Kreisel est né à Vienne d'une famille juive en 1922. En 1938, il a quitté son pays natal pour l'Angleterre et a été interné pendant dix-huit mois, au Canada, lors de la Deuxième Guerre mondiale. Après ses études à l'Université de Toronto, il devint professeur à l'Université de l'Alberta en 1947, et à partir de 1961 jusqu'à 1970, il a dirigé le Département d'anglais. De 1970 à 1975, il a été vice-recteur (universitaire), et a été nommé professeur hors rang en 1975, la plus haute distinction scientifique décernée par l'Université de l'Alberta à un membre de son professorat. Professeur adoré, il a transmis l'amour de la littérature à plusieurs générations d'étudiants, et il a été parmi les premiers à aborder l'expérience immigrante dans la littérature canadienne moderne. Il est décédé à Edmonton en 1991. Son œuvre comprend les romans, *The Rich Man* (1948) et *The Betrayal* (1964), et un recueil de nouvelles intitulé *The Almost Meeting* (1981). Son journal d'internement, accompagné d'articles critiques sur ses écrits, paraît dans *Another Country: Writings by and about Henry Kreisel* (1985).

La générosité du Professeur Kreisel est une source d'inspi-ration profonde quant au travail public et scientifique du CLC de sonder la grande diversité, complexité et qualité remar-quable des écrits au Canada. Le Centre adhère à l'importance qu'accordait de façon inaugurale Henry Kreisel à la connais-sance des littératures de son propre pays. C'est à sa mémoire que nous poursuivons une meilleure compréhension d'un monde difficile que la littérature peut nous aider à imaginer et transformer.

Le Centre de littérature canadienne a été créé en 2006 grâce au don directeur du bibliophile illustre edmontonien, le docteur Eric Schloss.

MARIE CARRIÈRE
Directrice, Centre de littérature canadienne
Edmonton, juin 2020

INTRODUCTION

JORDAN ABEL

I wanted to start out with one of the University of Alberta's territorial acknowledgements:

> The University of Alberta respectfully acknowledges that we are located on Treaty 6 territory, a traditional gathering place for diverse Indigenous Peoples including the Cree, Blackfoot, Metis, Nakota Sioux, Iroquois, Dene, Ojibway/ Saulteaux/Anishinaabe, Inuit, and many others whose histories, languages, and cultures continue to influence our vibrant community.

I also want to say thank you to the Canadian Literature Centre for inviting the renowned Leanne Betasamosake Simpson to deliver the 2020 Kreisel lecture.

I first encountered Leanne Simpson's work during my PHD program. I had been reading Indigenous writing almost exclusively, including a few wonderful books by folks like Eden Robinson, Daniel Heath Justice, Craig Womack, Linda Tuhiwai Smith, Lee Maracle, Gregory Scofield, Bonita Lawrence, Joyce Green, and Glen Coulthard. Actually, one of the very first essays I wrote during my PHD was about Glen Coulthard and Leanne Simpson. When I think back on it, I remember being completely enamoured by one of Simpson's arguments in *Dancing on Our Turtle's Back*. Simpson's argument came from the Anishnaabe idea that "one needs to be very, very careful with making judgments and with the act of criticism."[1] I think, if I understand the idea correctly, it's not so much that we can't or shouldn't critique anything, but that we need to be thinking more deeply on it before we act. Likewise, I remember being very surprised when I turned back to Coulthard's work only to find that most of *Red Skin, White Masks* seemed to offer very little beyond critique, and that in the conclusion of that book—when Coulthard finally moves away from critique and points towards the very difficult work of imaging a pathway forward—he turns to Leanne Simpson's vision of Indigenous resurgence as being a site of possibility for Indigenous futurity. In *Dancing on Our Turtle's Back*, Simpson writes that "critique and revelation cannot in and of themselves create the kinds of magnificent change our people are looking for," and that instead of spending all our time critiquing, we should be "spend[ing] an enormous amount of energy recovering and rebuilding."[2] Simpson's thinking here blew my mind. The idea that "one needs to be very, very careful with making judgments and with the act of criticism" challenged me to think outside of the usual structures and to try to do something generative.

The second time I encountered Leanne Simpson it was in person and in a much different context. I had just launched my third book, *Injun*, and Leanne and I were both at a reading in Vancouver. I can't recall exactly where, but it was somewhere downtown on what was probably a rainy night. I believe Leanne was reading from her first collection of short stories, poems, and songs, *Islands of Decolonial Love*, and I was performing my sound poetry from *Injun*. When we finally introduced ourselves to each other, it felt as though we already had known each other for a long time. I also remember very clearly that Leanne told me that when she had read my book *Injun* it sounded very different in her head than it did when I performed it. I am pretty sure I apologized for this. I think, for the lack of a better way to describe it, I was star-struck. After all, *Islands of Decolonial Love* was the book that everyone was talking about. Lee Maracle, for example, wrote of this book, "*Islands of Decolonial Love* is the sort of book I have been looking for all my life—the kind of book that is going to make me a good writer, a good listener, a good citizen—it is going to wake up everything that is brilliant in everyone that reads it." Richard Van Camp called the book "astounding storytelling" and "wonderous prose." He described *Islands of Decolonial Love* as "a constellation of galaxies that I never want to leave."[3]

I think no one would fault me for my love of Leanne Simpson's work. But I do have to admit it was very different to hear her work in this context, to think through her work in this context. In the academic context, I think that love was a bit more muted, a bit more reserved. Other academics were perhaps afraid to gush about how much they loved Simpson's work. But in the moment of that Vancouver reading, in the context of celebrating literature and creativity, I am not afraid to gush at all. That reading in Vancouver was an important moment for me where I got to share the stage with one of my favourite writers, and one that I will hold with me forever.

The third key time I encountered Leanne Simpson was during the New Constellations tour in Winnipeg. I had gotten sick just a few weeks before the tour began and decided not to get on the bus to travel through Edmonton and Calgary. Instead, I just decided to meet up with the tour in Winnipeg, where I had been hanging out as writer-in-residence at the University of Manitoba. I think I was invited on this tour as a poet, even though music really seemed to be the centre of this event, and when I got up on stage and read my poems, I felt very out of place, even if everyone was really quite kind. It's tough to be on the same stage as Jeremy Dutcher, Mob Bounce, John K. Samson, Jason Collett, and July Talk. I am, after all, mostly just a poet. But Leanne Simpson was there not as an Indigenous philosopher or even as a creative writer but as a musician. She had a band. She had a guitar. She was—and is—also a rock star. When I was talking to her after the show, it was clear that she had literally been living the rock star life in a tour bus with a bunch of other musicians, fighting for a shower whenever they stopped in a new town.

This is all to say that Leanne Simpson is an absolute gem, and I think we would be hard-pressed to find anyone nearly as talented across so many different fields and genres.

Just listen for a second to what some folks have been saying about Leanne Simpson's work. Thomas King, for example, writes, "Leanne is a gifted writer who brings passion and commitment to her storytelling and who has demonstrated an uncommon ability to manage an impressive range of genres from traditional storytelling to critical analysis, from poetry to the spoken word, from literary and social activism to song-writing. She is, in my opinion, one of the more articulate and engaged voices of her generation."[4]

Likewise, Waubgeshig Rice writes,

Leanne Simpson is a masterful storyteller and an
integral Indigenous voice in modern literature. Her work
over the years has eloquently and powerfully captured the
unique experiences of the first peoples of Turtle Island...
With precise craft, [Simpson's writing] explores the many
complicated facets of the contemporary Indigenous struggle
to maintain tradition in a rapidly changing environment.
The use of Anishinaabe language and custom in the prose
and poetry resonates loudly and invokes a great sense
of pride. Meanwhile, the challenge of balancing urban and
reserve life explored in the pieces is easily relatable and
can provide a crucial window into the experience for
non-Indigenous readers.[5]

I am absolutely in awe of what Simpson has been able
to accomplish, and I think we are extraordinarily lucky to
continue to read, to continue to listen to, and to continue
to think with this absolutely brilliant human being. As
Katherena Vermette has said, "Simpson is a master lyricist,
a captivating storyteller, and a true gift to us all."[6] Please
welcome Leanne Simpson.

The writer cannot be a mere storyteller; he cannot be a mere teacher; he cannot merely x-ray society's weaknesses, its ills, its perils. He or she [or they] must be actively involved shaping its present and its future.

—KEN SARO-WIWA, "Trying Times"

I am Michi Saagiig Nishnaabeg or Ojibway and our home is the north shore of Lake Ontario, roughly in between the cities of Toronto and Ottawa.[1]

My particular understanding of life comes from this part of the world.

It comes from this Michi Saagiig Nishnaabeg practice of life, living in deep relationality to the land, the water, the plants, the animals, and the peoples of Kina Gchi Nishnaabeg Ogaming—the place where we all live and work together. It comes from Nayaano Nibiimaang Gichigamiing, the Great Lakes. It comes from maple sugar bushes carrying and filtering water from the soil, combining it with light and converting it to sweet sugar. It comes from lakeshores full of minomiin, or wild rice, gathering strength in mid-July and moving from floating form to standing upright. It comes from black bears that wake up in Makwa Giizis, February, turn in their dens on beds of blueberry branches and then settle back into fasting and dreaming for a few more weeks.

This land has taught me that Nishnaabeg life is continual, reciprocal, and reflective. Sometimes, it is a critical engagement with my ancestors, those yet to be born, and the nations of beings with whom I share land. It is a living constellation of co-resistance with all of the anti-colonial peoples and the worlds they build. This land has taught me that Nishnaabeg life is a persistent world-building process, despite of and in spite of the constant imposition of the colonial machinery of elimination.

This procedure for Indigenous life and Indigenous living is one that Indigenous Peoples used long before our existence ever depended upon our ability to resist and survive the violence of capitalism, heteropatriarchy, and expansive dispossession.

My ancestors woke up each morning and created an Nishnaabeg world. They animated their political system of governance and diplomacy, they built their collective philo-sophical and ethical understandings, they made processes for solving conflict and re-establishing balance, and they built their economy with the consent of the plant and animal nations. They built, maintained, and nurtured systems for sharing knowledge and taking care of each other. They worked collec-tively to produce, reproduce, replicate, amplify, and share Nishnaabeg life, because if they did not, Nishnaabeg worlds would not exist.

They were makers.

They got up each morning and they worked hard, not the white man wage-labour Monday-to-Friday, nine-to-five, kind of work. Not the kind of work where you outsource the labour of living so you can do something more important, but the kind of work that values, above all else, the way one lives. They got up, worked hard all day long in a way that brought forth more life.[2]

This algorithm of living, theory and praxis seamlessly intertwined and relationally responsive to each other, is

generated through intimate relations with Michi Saagiig
Nishnaabeg land, land that is constructed and defined by
our dynamic intellectual, spiritual, emotional, and physical
relationality.

Living as a creative act.

Self-determination, consent, kindness, and freedom
practiced daily in all our relations.

Practices replicated over and over.

Making as the material basis for experiencing and
influencing the world.

Living with the purpose of generating continual life.

Our infrastructure for life was relationships, not
institutions.

Our orientation for life was internationalist. We shared
space and time with plant and animal nations and different
Indigenous nations mostly without the use of enclosures and
violence.

We did not bank capital to protect us against hard times.
We had interdependent relationships with animal and plants
nations, other human families and neighbouring Indigenous
nations. In times of difficulty, we relied upon this practice of
relational diplomacy and the words it creates to survive, with
the understanding that in return we would in also take care
of their worlds.[3]

We have always been intellectual and artistic peoples.
We have always had theory, meaning, philosophy, aesthetic
principles, and those things were considered and celebrated
on nights like this, through the practice of storytelling.

My people are constant storytellers throughout the day,
and throughout the seasons. Stories are the fabric of daily
life. The sonics of story pulls one into a space, where worlds
are fully embodied experience. The sound is the connector
to emotions and intellect beyond one's own body, it is a

connector to all of the relations that make up the land. The land holds story, from this is the place where when you were two you got stung by a bee and fell into the beaver pond; to before that monster cottage was built on that island your great-grandparents always camped on their way to town; to remember the time Nanabush transformed into a tree but forgot that one body part; to the place where you first tasted smart berries; and look, there are geese flying overhead in a v.

Stories not only fill our worlds, they make our worlds, but only if you have the skills to find meaning in oral literature. But only if story lives and breathes inside of you. But only if you wrap stories around you like a blanket and take them out to consider from time to time.

Telling stories is a foundational practice of Indigenous Peoples.

The practice of telling stories fills the interstitial spaces of worlds with recognition and affirmation with all of that generative and degenerative energy. It is a practice of listening with one's open heart to the sound of Nishnaabeg across time and space in all of our manifestations.

The practice of telling stories is the practice of generating a diversity of meanings. It is a practice of deep relationality, not a looking at, but a looking with or a looking through or a *thinking through together*.

The practice of telling stories is a practice of contracting and releasing sound across scales—articulating our individual experiences, relating them to collective experiences and generating systemic critique. More important than the telling is the culture of listening.

The practice of telling stories is the practice of constantly building Nishnaabeg worlds while simultaneously living in them.

We are bodies made of stories and connection—hubs in the network of Indigenous living, and our practice of telling stories is one of the reasons that I'm here, today, in spite of centuries of colonial violence.

In February of 2020 we witnessed a phenomenal expression of Indigenous international diplomacy as Indigenous Peoples across Canada have mobilized in solidarity with the Wet'suwet'en hereditary chiefs and their clans in the form of rallies, round dances, teach-ins, benefit concerts, sit-ins, and of course, blockades.

We have also witnessed the usual vitriol white racism in backlash to those expressions of solidarity, online, in the media, at the frontlines, and from Canada's so-called leaders.

The Wet'suwet'en hereditary chiefs have repeatedly stated that there is no access to their lands without their consent, and over the past two decades, they have done everything possible within current structures to protect their lands. When the RCMP invaded their territory to enforce a court injunction to make way for the construction of the pipeline, they asked us for our support in protecting their land and their peoples from the Coastal GasLink pipeline.[4]

Canada has a long present and a long history of ignoring Indigenous consent when it comes to resource extraction on our territories and they have always undermined our self-determination to decide what is best for our peoples and our lands.

Canada has a long present and a long history of ignoring Black consent when it comes to environmental harm, self-determination, freedom, and the proliferation of Black life.

Kathryn Yusoff writes in *A Billion Black Anthropocenes or None*, "If the Anthropocene proclaims a sudden concern with the exposures of environmental harm to white liberal communities, it does so in the wake of histories in which these harms have been knowingly exported to black and brown communities under the rubric of civilization, progress, modernization and capitalism. The Anthropocene might seem to offer a dystopic future that laments the end of the world, but imperialism and ongoing (settler) colonialism have been ending worlds for as long as they have been in existence."[5]

Indeed, as poet, novelist, and playwright, M. NourbeSe Philip writes, North America is founded upon two genocides, Black peoples and Indigenous Peoples.[6]

The Wet'suwet'en hereditary chiefs are teaching the world a crucial message about consent.

They've used the Canadian courts in the landmark *Delgamuukw* decision, they've educated the public on speaking tours, videos, a website, and camp tours, and they have built the alternative—a land immersive community with cabins, a pit house, bunkhouses, and a healing centre at the Unist'ot'en camp. A tremendous expression of life-giving Wet'suwet'en law, politics, economy, and love.

A Wet'suwet'en world, where no means no, with Indigenous bodies and Indigenous land.

Yellowknives Dene political theorist Glen Coulthard, in a blog post titled "For Indigenous Nations to Live, Capitalism Must Die," posted during the height of Idle No More writes that the state has always placed limits on Indigenous efforts to protect our lands. There are clear demarcations between moral and "legitimate" forms of defending our rights and morally "illegitimate" methods—deemed so because of their disruptive or extra-legal character.[7]

"Legitimate" forms of protecting our rights are usually negotiations between state-sanctioned Aboriginal leadership and the Crown, along with symbolic acts of

peaceful and non-disruptive demonstrations sanctioned by
Canadian law.

Morally "illegitimate" tactics are forms of protest and
direct action that are less mediated and sometimes more
disruptive like slowing traffic, temporary blockades,
and the re-occupation of Indigenous lands through the
establishment of reclamation sites that also serve to disrupt,
if not entirely block, access to Indigenous territories by state
and capital for prolonged periods of time.

As Coulthard writes, most often, "morally illegitimate"
activities get branded in the media in a negative manner, as
reactionary, threatening, dangerous and disruptive.[8]

Mohawk scholar Audra Simpson, in *Mohawk Interruptus:
Political Life across the Borders of Settler States*, provides
us with another important lens through which to view
blockades: refusal. In considering the Iroquois Nationals
Lacrosse Team's refusal of Canadian passports to travel to
international competition, Simpson writes,

> What does it mean to refuse a passport—what some
> consider to be a gift or a right, the freedom of mobility and
> residency? What does it mean to say no to these things,
> or to wait until your terms have been met for agreement,
> for a reversal of recognition, or a conferral of rights?
> What happens when we refuse what all (presumably)
> "sensible" people perceive as good things? What does this
> refusal do to politics, to sense, to reason? When we add
> Indigenous peoples to this question, the assumptions and
> the histories that structure what is perceived to be "good"
> (and utilitarian goods themselves) shift and stand in stark
> relief. The positions assumed by people who refuse "gifts"
> may seem reasoned, sensible and in face deeply correct.[9]

Indigenous blockades are indeed a refusal of the dominant
political and economic systems of Canada. They are a refusal
to accept erasure, banishment, disappearance, and death
from our homelands.[10] They are indeed an amplification and
centring of Indigenous political economies—Indigenous
forms of governance, economy, production, and exchange.
They are indeed a resurgence of social and political practices,
ethics and knowledge systems, and in this way they are a
generative refusal.

Lakota scholar Nick Estes writes,

Ancestors of Indigenous resistance didn't merely fight
against settler colonialism; they fought *for* Indigenous life
and just relations with human and nonhuman relatives,
and with the earth. When Custer and his men descended
on the sun dance at Greasy Grass, the ancestors were
dancing, as they have since time immemorial, to make the
tree of life in Black Elk's vision bloom, and to ensure the
rebirth of their people and the earth. In 2016, as construction
of the Black Snake—the Dakota Access pipeline—began,
they danced again, this time on the shore at Oceti Sakowin
Camp and at Sacred Stone to protect Mni Sose (the Missouri
River) and Unci Maka (Grandmother Earth). Indigenous
resistance is not a one-time event. It continually asks: What
proliferates in the absence of empire? Thus, it defines
freedom not as the absence of settler colonialism, but as
the amplified presence of Indigenous life and just relations
with human and nonhuman relatives and with the earth.[11]

In reality, behind the barricades, whether the blockades are
enacted on Anishinaabeg land at Grassy Narrows, Dakota
land at Standing Rock at the port of Vancouver, or at

Unist'ot'ten, blockades are rich sites of Indigenous life, of a radical resurgence.

In the spaces behind the barricades, you'll find parents with children. You'll find Elders. You'll encounter ceremony, sacred fires, and language learning. Art making. Singing. Drumming. Storytelling.

You'll find an ethic of care as harvesters and cooks engage in a bush economy to feed the frontlines alongside spiritual leaders, nurses, and medics taking care of the people. You will notice a mobilized network of support and solidarity extending well beyond the barricades.

You will witness the re-emergence of political leaders based not on a band council election, but upon Indigenous practices of deep relationality.

You will enter a collective embodiment of Indigenous legal practices.

You will hear the sound of political, intellectual, and spiritual engagement in these rich sites of knowledge production, and you'll see Indigenous anti-colonial theory generated through embodied collective practice.

You will witness a radically different political existence and ethical orientation, in spite of the dominance of colonialism. Existences and orientations that are operating upon a different premise than that the politics and economy of extraction.

Living as a creative act.

Self-determination, consent, kindness, and freedom practiced daily in all our relations.

Practices, replicated over and over.

Making as the material basis for experiencing and influencing the world.

Living with the purpose of generating continual life.

Nbwaakawin.[12]

Tonight, I want to step away from the usual ways blockades are portrayed in the media and are understood by the majority of Canadians. I want to spend some time thinking about this practice of the blockade in a different way, in an Nishnaabeg way. In an Nishnaabeg way that is in conversation with the Wet'suwet'en, Nehiyawak, Blackfoot, Stoney Nakota, Métis peoples, and the Indigenous brilliance of this particular place, in the spirit of Indigenous internationalism. I want to share the brilliance of my relative, the beaver.

According to the *Edmonton Journal*, you all have between 1,300 and 1,600 beavers living in this city, which beats Calgary's 200 and Winnipeg's 100.[13] I think we have the glorious nature of the North Saskatchewan River to thank for that, which means we have the brilliance of the beaver among us tonight.

In colonial minds, the beaver is "nature's engineer." The earliest forester. The first hydrologist. The original industry. "No one has had more impact on the environment than beavers, except for humans," the zhaaganash boast.

In 1975 the beaver became an emblem of Canada as a symbol of its sovereignty because the first Europeans in Indigenous territories saw the beaver, not as a relative, but as a money-making attraction to supply the continent with nifty felt hats.

Two hundred years of making beavers into accessories led to their near extermination, and now beavers are mostly known as a nuisance and an inconvenience.

But this Indigenous land, this Indigenous water, these Indigenous bodies house centuries of oral literature and embodied practice that know different.

The Seven Ancestor teachings, often referred to as the Seven Grandfather Teachings or, in my region, Kokum Dibaajimowinan, are foundational practices that guide Nishnaabeg all of our relations. They were gifted to the Nishnaabeg by Seven Ancestors, a group of loving Elders and advisors that taught a young child these practices as recorded in one of our Sacred Stories. The practices were intended to provide peace and a good life for all living beings on earth.[14] These practices include Aakde'ewin, the art of having a strong heart or courage; Debwewin, the practice of listening to the sound of one's heart, truth, or sincerity; Mnaadendiwin, the art of living with respect; Zaagidewin, the practice of loving; Dbadendiziwin, living with humility; Nbwaakawin, the practice of knowledge; and Kaazhaadiziwin, the art of embodying the six other teachings or kindness.[15] Each of these practices is represented by an animal relation who best embodies those practices, and the animal nations carry a body of stories that deepen our understandings of these concepts and how to live them.

According to Curve Lake Elder Doug Williams, there is another source of knowledge that deepens our understanding of Kokum Dibaajimowinan, and that is our Grandparents. He explained to me that one of the responsibilities of Grandparents, often Grandmothers, was to tell children narratives about particular individuals in their families or community that best embodied these practices. Each young person would then have a body of knowledge through stories that connected them intimately to their family, and connected them to the land through the animal stories.[16]

Odawa Elder and language expert Shirley Williams explained to me that the beaver's responsibility, knowledge, or wisdom means "the art of kindness in knowledge." It means to put others before yourself. In other words, you can meet your own needs and think about yourself after you have thought about your family and community. Kindness in the practice of knowledge is the highest form of wisdom, one that needs care, and humility. Wisdom can be used for destruction or to promote more life—one must be careful.[17]

In many versions of the Nishnaabeg Seven Ancestor teachings, beavers—or in Anishinaabemowin, Amik, plural Amikwag—represents Nbwaakawin, the practice of wisdom.[18]

I want to think about that for a minute.

Out of all of the beings that make up life on this planet, to my ancestors, Amikwag best embodied the politics and ethical practices of wisdom.

Now there are some pretty cool features of the beaver and, as a sporty person, I'm immediately attracted to waterproof fur, the original Gortex. Webbed feet for efficiency in the pool. A third eyelid in the form of a nictitating clear membrane that moves over theirs eyes and acts as swim goggles you cannot loose. Orange and ever-growing teeth with iron in them, perfect for gnawing and not susceptible to yellow stains.

Then I remember, for the Nishnaabeg, it is not necessarily our cool and sporty features that make us who we are—it is what we do and how we live in relation to all other forms of life.

Amikwag build lodges, canals, and dams. And, of course, the longest beaver dam in the world is located north of here in Treaty 8 and measures 850 metres long.

Amikwag build dams.

Dams that create deep pools and channels that don't freeze, creating winter worlds for their fish relatives. Deep pools and channels that drought-proof the landscape. Dams that make wetlands full of moose, deer and elk food, cooling stations, places to hide calves, and muck to keep the flies away. Dams that open spaces in the canopy so sunlight increases, making warm and shallow aquatic habitat around the edges of the pond for amphibians and insects. Dams that create plunge pools on the downstream side for juvenile fish, gravel for spawning, and homes and food for birds. And who is the first back after a fire to start the regeneration? Amikwag.

Amik is a world builder.

Amik is the one that brings the water.

Amik is the one that brings forth more life.

Amik is the one that works continuously with water and land and animal and plant nations and consent and diplomacy to create worlds, to create *shared* worlds.

Prior to contact with white people, it is estimated that Mikinaakong was home to between 60 and 400 million beavers. That is three to five beavers for every kilometre of stream or river. That is, a beaver in nearly every headwater stream in North America. Biologists call the beaver a keystone species—a species so important to an ecosystem that without it the ecosystem would collapse. A species that continually creates habitats and food sources for other beings. Families that filter and purify water. Clans that replenish the soil with nutrients. Communities that manage spring floods and water temperatures. A nation that continually gives.

A beaver dam, a blockade:

Life giving.

Generative.

Affirmative.

A world-building place, governed by deep relationality.

An expansive fantastical sharing of space.

A network of life-generating blockades that built and maintained the ecosystems that Nishnaabeg, Nehiyawak, and Dene,[19] for instance, lived as part of for thousands and thousands of years.

Nbwaakawin.

Land-based politics grounded in a sustained and nurturing relationship with the natural world and in protecting nature is a means of protecting ourselves.

—ZOÉ SAMUDZI and WILLIAM C. ANDERSON,
As Black As Resistance: Find the Conditions for Liberation

ONE

Now beaver infrastructure is quite a bit different than
colonial and capitalistic infrastructure. Michi Saagiig
Nishnaabeg scholar Madeline Whetung, from Curve Lake
First Nation, has written about this in a paper called
"(En)gendering Shoreline Law: Nishnaabeg Relational
Politics along the Trent Severn Waterway."[20]

Whetung writes that in 1833, in Michi Saagiig Nishnaabeg
territory on the north shore of Lake Ontario, a group of six
white-settler men conspired to build a canal system of locks
and dams connecting Lake Ontario or Chi'Nibish to Georgian
Bay or Odawa Wiikwedong. This was the Nishnaabeg 401—
a major canoe thoroughfare that had been used for centuries
to quickly travel between the two big lakes. But powerful,
upper-class capitalists never liked canoeing as much as we
did, and so a canal system in their minds was a more efficient
way to bring settlers, and capitalism, to our territory—
without our knowledge and without our consent.[21]

Today, a monument stands at the Bobcaygeon lock that
celebrates the canal's purpose to "open up the interior of

the province, and to promote agriculture, lumbering and commerce."[22]

Indeed, Doug Williams, the Curve Lake Elder Madeline and I both work with, credits the construction of the Trent Severn Waterway as a devastating and destructive blow to Michi Saagiig Nishnaabeg life, leading to the extermination of salmon and eels from our territory, flooded burial grounds and camp sites, the decline of fish and animal relatives, the near destruction of minomiin—the cornerstone of our food system—and an overwhelming increase in settlers.[23]

Two dams. Two very different outcomes.

The Trent Severn Waterway, a negation.

The beaver dam, both a negation and an affirmation.

In our thinking through of this idea of a blockade together, I'm going to try and deepen our understandings by sharing with you four beaver stories.

The first story takes place a long, long time ago to the time of the very first beaver dam. In the time where beavers were giant.

Mewizha. Mewizha. Mewizha.

I've heard Giant Beaver stories in Nishnaabeg, Nehiyawak, and Dene homelands, and according to scientists, Castoroides lived in the Pleistocene era and were two metres long, weighing about one hundred kilograms. Beavers roughly the size of black bears.

Now scientists don't know if Giant Beavers made dams, but the Nishnaabeg do, and we have the stories as evidence.

What follows is my version of the story that was told by Sam Snake, Elijah Yellowhead, Alder York, and Annie King from the Chippewas of Rama, Mnjikaning First Nation, and was originally recorded and complied by Emerson and David Coatsworth in *The Adventures of Nanabush*, published in 1979.[24]

Chi'Diplomacy

Call-out culture is exhausting and no one knows this better than Giant Beaver and Nanabush. These two have been trading witty and not-so-witty barbs back and forth all over the country and it's been so long neither of them can remember what the original fight was about. But Owah, did they both ever get a spike in followers.

Nanabush had been stalking Giant Beaver around the internet for months before they lost their trail completely.

It took a few days of consulting with their followers to figure out if Nanabush had been blocked or if Giant Beaver had shut down all their accounts and disappeared from the internet completely.

When it was decided that it was the later, and all that was left was the quiet, Nanabush also logged off and went back to the land with Nokomis to find solace.

Nokomis set their net in the narrows between the two lakes, Gichi Gaming, which you might know as Lake Superior, and Odawa Gaming, which you might know as Lake Huron. They built a lodge made out of saplings and bark and lined with cedar branches. They wove mats out of cattails for sleeping. They ate grouse for dinner, made mint and cedar tea, and picked medicine until it was time to check their nets. Then Nokomis tried to teach Nanabush how to smoke whitefish.

Nanabush was pretty busy though reading a lot of books because they were studying for their comprehensive exams and that is no joke. At least in certain contexts.

Things were going along pretty good for these two. So good in fact that Nanabush even considered shutting down their socials for good.

Nanabush and Nokomis were so relaxed in fact, they didn't notice it happening at first. Small, incremental change can be like that. But each day, the water level was rising, ever so slightly.

Nanabush knew immediately that Giant Beaver was back online under fake accounts causing trouble.

Nokomis knew immediately that Giant Beaver had dammed the head of the lake and was still building.

Nanabush fired up Twitter, Facebook, Snapchat, and Instagram.

Nokomis found the dam.

Nanabush clicked, posted, retweeted, and regrammed.

Nokomis sat on top.

Nanabush memed.

Nokomis waited.

Nanbush typed in A-M-I-K-1 serendipity style and opened all Giant Beaver's accounts.

Nokomis waited.

Nanabush opened all the platforms screen after screen after screen, finger on delete.

Nokomis waited.

Nanabush deleted each post seconds after they appeared.

Nokomis waited.

Nanabush deleted.

Giant Beaver burst through.

Nokomis grabbed onto their tail and held on.

Nokomis hung on. For two days. Through the night and past exhaustion. Through the day and past pain. And when they couldn't hold on any longer, Giant Beaver burst free drilling through the dam to break away.

Nokomis felt like a complete failure. A fraud of a Nokomis.

Nanabush rubbed their back.

Nokomis looked up, and saw Giant Beaver's dam, blasted apart, forming the spectacular 30,000 islands in Georgian Bay, or Odawa Wiikwedong.

Giant Beaver headed east through Kina Gchi Nishnaabeg
ogaming, and was gently carried by Kchi Ziibi to the ocean.

Nanabush ran after them, but it was too late. So Nanabush
called out:

"I want to be your friend."

Giant Beaver stopped.

Thought.

Considered.

And then Giant Beaver returned to Nanabush and
Nokomis to figure out how to use their beaver skills for good.
Which they did, and all it required was a little patience,
a little resistance, some community, and a considerable
reduction in size to the Amik we know and love today.

Nbwaakawin.

Her heart was beaded from
smoke tanned hands that could
turn struggle into beauty.

—TUNCHAI REDVERS, *Fireweed*

TWO

In my culture, spring is the time for fasting, and fasting is not an easy thing nowadays. We aren't used to being alone with quiet. Most of us are lucky enough to not have to go without food or water for long periods of time. Our reality is one infused with the electric of anxiety, and our bodies are ready for fight or flight when neither is the reality. So fasting, while our spiritual leaders insist on its importance, colonial realities as per usual present some particular challenges. Many Elders see those challenges and offer support and a certain fluidity around the practice designed, I think, to teach us slowly and gently the skills needed to complete four days and four nights. Few of us have the drive and commitment needed to accomplish this because the benefit at the end is entirely collective, wholly internal, and without accolades.

When Wiijiiwagan decided to fast, they planned for these particular challenges years in advance. They practiced. They did the things they had been taught to do regularly, even though, even though, and so when the day came, Nokomis put the charcoal on their face in the Nishnaabe way, and they began.

It isn't ethically appropriate to speak specifically about our practices of fasting, or what happened in this particular fast other than to repeat what those have gone before me have said. John Binesi (Kaagige Binesi or Forever Bird), from what is now known as Fort William First Nation, told this story to William Jones and it was originally published in 1919, known as "The Woman Who Married a Beaver."[25] William Jones was a Mesquaki anthropologist and he recorded many Ojibwe stories from the western part of our territory in our language. In Kaagige Binesi's published and translated version of the story, he says that during the fast, the faster, which we will call Wiijiiwagan, meaning partner or companion, met a person who invited them to their home. Wiijiiwagan agreed. The home was beautiful. Food and clothing were plentiful, and, in time, Wiijiiwagan consented to become this person's partner.

When everyone agreed and the decision to be together was made, Wiijiiwagan lost all memories of their parents and their previous life.

The two had a beautiful life together.

They had four children, and the family was able to meet its needs through hard work. They had lots to eat. Things were good.

Now Wiijiiwagan's partner would sometimes leave their home for periods of time to go and visiting. Sometimes, they would take the children. Sometimes, they would go alone. Always, they came back with beautiful and useful gifts— tobacco, clothing, kettles, knives, and bowls. Sometimes, friends would come and visit their lodge too, but they never entered the lodge.

At some point in the relationship, as happens in all long-term relationships, Wiijiiwagan became aware that their partner was not exactly the same as them in body, spirit, and in mind. I believe we have all had this sort of experience. But at this point in time, for Wiijiiwagan, they realized that they had entered into a relationship, a partnership with a beaver, Amik.

Now let's revisit that previous paragraph in light of this new knowledge that Wiijiiwagan is in a relationship with a beaver.

Wiijiiwagan's beaver partner would sometimes leave their home for periods of time to go and visiting. Sometimes, they would take the children. Sometimes, they would go alone. Always, they came back with beautiful and useful gifts—tobacco, clothing, kettles, knives, and bowls. Sometimes, friends would come and visit their lodge too, but they never entered the lodge.

In Nishnaabewin, it is obvious what is happening here. But it is not so obvious in a Western world view, so allow me to explain. In Nishnaabewin, the spiritual world is alive and influencing, and it is really the main event. The physical world, which most of us usually inhabit, is sort of a detritus for what happens in the spirit world.

When the beaver goes away to visit, they are being hunted by the Nishnaabeg. They are consenting to giving up their bodies to help the Nishnaabeg feed their families.

When they return, they have been killed in the physical world, and the gifts they are bringing—the tobacco, clothing, kettles, knives, and bowls—are gifts of reciprocity from the Nishnaabeg. This is an ethical exchange because the beaver does not have to give up their life, they do so with consent. The gifts are an expression of international diplomacy between the Nishnaabeg and the beavers.

Towards the end of Amik's life, Amik asked Wiijiiwagan to speak to the visiting one the next time they came by, so that they could return to the human world.

Wiijiiwagan did, and they returned to the Nishnaabeg. Wiijiiwagan shared their story of life with Amik and asked the Nishnaabeg to respect their relation.

This is such an interesting story for me with a layered and complex intelligence embedded in it. My Turtle Mountain Ojibwe colleague and friend Heidi Kiiwetinepinesiik Stark has written a wonderful paper about this story called "Respect, Responsibility, and Renewal: The Foundations of Anishnaabe Treaty Making with the United States and Canada."[26]

This story takes place during a very prosperous time for both the Beaver nation and the Nishnaabeg.

And we visited each other regularly. We gifted the beavers with our most precious belongings and the beavers gifted the Nishnaabeg with their lives in the human world, so that we could feed our families.

You see, there are always worlds on top of worlds, worlds underneath worlds, worlds intertwined with worlds. It's a sort of Nishnaabeg String Theory.

There is an intricate, ongoing reciprocity here practiced between individuals, families, and nations that is facilitated by visiting.

Stark also argues, and I would agree, that this story "recounts the forging and functioning of a treaty relationship between Nishnaabeg and the beavers."[27]

Nishnaabeg responsibilities included tobacco, gifts, returning the bones of the beavers to water to renew the treaty, and speaking out to protect beaver habitats and worlds when necessary. The beavers in turn gave up their lives in the human world and then returned to the beaver world.

Both nations lived without want.

Both nations valued the practices of consent, sharing, care, sovereignty, and self-determination.

Both nations shared time, space, water, and land.

Stark writes,

"The Woman Who Married a Beaver" is a powerful story of transformation that sheds light on how the Anishinaabe understood treaty making. The young girl is literally transformed into a beaver. Through this change, she learns how important the principles of respect, responsibility and renewal are for a healthy and beneficial relationship to continue between the Anishinaabe and the beavers. She brought these lessons back to the Anihsinaabe when she returned to her people. These principles were and remain foundational to the development and sustainability of mutually beneficial relationships. Treaty making was about making relationships. They were not mere agreements that ceded one thing in exchange for another. Treaties bound nations to one another. They carried commitments that did not end with the exchange of land or annuities. These agreements connected people. Treaties were a vision for what a multinational society could entail.[28]

As both Whetung and Stark point out, when the white-settler men built the dams, canals, and locks of the Trent Severn Waterway, they did so in violation of Michi Saagiig Nishnaabeg and beaver practices of consent, reciprocity, respect, and renewal.[29] They did so in violation of Michi Saagiig Nishnaabeg and beaver diplomacy. They did so with complete disregard of the intimate political, economic, and ethical relationality that created these Nishnaabeg and beaver worlds.

A negation, without the possibility of an affirmation. An ending of life.

Let's think back to Giant Beaver for a second, and that first blockade, and let's just appreciate how generative it was. Let's just give thanks to Nokomis and Nanabush for not arresting Giant Beaver, destroying the blockade, and going back to business as usual.

Nbwaakawin.

For a century, no one spoke of the extinction of joy.[30]

—BILLY-RAY BELCOURT,
NDN Coping Mechanisms: Notes from the Field

THREE

In 2006, Steve Daniels, an electronic artist and past director of new media in the RTA School of Media at Ryerson University, created an installation called *anaBlog*.

anaBlog is an electro-mechanical community blog originally developed as a site-specific interactive installation for Blink, an annual exhibition held during Artsweek in Peterborough, Ontario. Part confessional, part message board, part soapbox, *anaBlog* is a DIY network that stands at the intersections of private and public space, personal and community standards, revelation and surveillance, graffiti and communication, vandalism and intervention. Mimicking the internet but physically structured around a clothesline, *anaBlog* is a playful examination of the web phenomenon of anonymously bearing one's soul in a public space.[31]

The third story riffs off this installation and is titled AnabLog.

AnabLog

Amik thinks we all need better communication
Amik thinks things would go better if we spent
more time, face to face,
in community.

but. but.
who has the time?

but. but.
who wants to see tweets in person?

but. but.
who wants to know
the mediocre parts no one posts
when we already have to live life?
hmmm?

well Amik is a maker of things
if nothing else.

and Jia Tolentino says virtual signaling is the new black.[32]

and muskrat mounds made of iPhone 5s
do have a particular shimmer.

so. so.

Amik installs an old school clothesline
between two trees
with a big pole in the middle
for extra support.

They build it in the cafe
because that's where everyone goes to drink
Mochaccinos anyway and
they install that old school clothesline
between two trees
right between all those tables and stump chairs.

They get motors and wire and pulleys from the dump,
and wooden clothes pins from the hippies and whamo.
AnabLog.

Each table has its own motor and string
and you post your note with the clothes pin
and then put it UP ON THE LINE for everyone to see.

Makwa arrives first crushes blueberries to make a print with
their middle finger up, and they put it up on the line.

Ma'iingan comes in and calls out Makwa for offensive
language and rips that print right off the line.

Tom King shows up and writes,

Tell me.
Tell me, who is left to hate?
Surely there is someone new,
        someone missed
        the first time through.

Tell me.
Shall we circle round
        and bring our wicked selves
        to ground?

Tell me.
Tell me.[33]

and he puts it up on the line.

Mashkode-bizhiki writes,
Humility is missing and murdered. FROM MASHKODE-
BIZHIKI

And puts it up on the line.

Buffalo writes,
mazin means
fancy,
figured,
an image.

aabik means
mineral,
rock,
metal
solid.

iwebinan means
forcefully by hard fling,
throwing
or shove by hand.

mazinaabikiwebinan. computer or typewriter. FROM
MASHKODE-BIZHIKI

And puts it up on the line.

Mashkode-bizhiki writes,

The sound of stealing kids is dead silence. FROM
MASHKODE-BIZHIKI

And puts it up on the line.

Sabe writes,

This isn't having the impact you think it is having.

And puts it up on the line.

Mashkode-bizhiki writes,

Omimii, the EXTINCT passenger pigeon. FROM
MASHOKODE-BIZHIKI

And puts it up on the line.

Giniw writes,

the settling
silence
of 2.9 billion
missing
and murdered
birds
since 1970,

and puts it up on the line.

Giniw writes,
2 out of 5 Baltimore Orioles

9 out of 10 Evening Grosbeaks

6 out of 10 Wood Thrushes

2 out of 5 Barn Swallows

3 out of 4 Eastern Meadowlarks

1 out of 4 of all Bineshiinyag

and puts it up on the line.

Giniw writes,
rookeries of 10,000 nests
flocks a mile wide,
300 miles long
taking 14 hours of dark skies
to pass.

Imagine.

And puts it up on the line.

Amik writes,
the internet negates humility #Mashkode-bizhikisays

And puts it up on the line.

Ma'iingan posts:
the emperor has no clothes #Amik

And puts it up on the line.

Ginebig posts:
Giniw is self serving.

And puts it up on the line.

Mooz follows with:
Amik is plagiarism.

And puts it up on the line.

Esiban writes,
if Amik hadn't built the selfie station at the Edmonton
airport I never would have gone there thinking it was a real
lodge.

And puts it up on the line.

Zhigaag writes,
Amik has a gross relationship with muskrat.

And puts it up on the line.

Aandeg writes,
Amik isn't really an Amik.

And puts it up on the line.

Amik takes a photo of their Authentic Eastern Woodland
Beaver Card and puts it up on the line.

Sabe writes $(C_2H_4)_n$ the formula for polyethylene and puts it up on the line.

Adik scotch tapes Makwa's obscene paw print back together and puts it up on the line.

Birch rewrites Ma'iingan's post about Makwa being obscene and adds #violence #solidarity #ibelieve

Waawaashkeshi takes a photo of Mikinaak at the cafe doing nothing and puts it up on the line along with a #complacent and #gross.

Mikinaak never goes to the cafe again.

Amik visits Makwa in person, face to face, and gifts them Amik's castoreum.

Amik visits Giniw in person, face to face, and gifts them Amik's tail.

Amik visits Mashkode-bizhiki in person, face to face, and gifts them Amik's front teeth.

Amik visits Sabe in person, face to face, and gifts them Amik's hide.

Amik visits Ma'iingan in person, face to face, and gifts them Amik's meat and bones.

Amik visits Mikinaak in person, face to face, and gifts them Amik's brains.

Amik sneaks back to the cafe in the dead of night, gnaws down the poles, cuts the line, takes the motors back to the dump, and then lies down and leaves this world.

Omiimi sings:

calling out
calling in
you're not fooling me

tethered to the kinship
of disassociated
zeros and ones

shining your crown
of neoliberal
likes

yelling the loudest
in the
empty room

gathering
followers
like berries

feeding
fish
to insecurity

sliding
into
reckless moment
after reckless moment

we witness:

too many holes in your hide
the broken skin of a canoe
the tightening of a mind
tracks, leading nowhere.

at the
beach
we build a fire

sit in our
own
silence

peel off
blue
light

lie back
on
frozen
waves

breath
in
sharp air

warm
into
each other

careful moment
after careful moment.[34]

sometimes that little one
who lives with the stars
looks down
and just
feels proud of us.

Nbwaakawin.

The only thing stronger than actual film, as far as getting things across is actual, direct action. That's direct action, whether you're actually going out there, putting your body out there where people have to react against it.[35]

—WILLIE DUNN, in CBC Music, *60 Years of Indigenous Music Game Changers*

FOUR

One of the markers of aging if you are an Indigenous parent is when your kids hear about the protest before you do.

This recently happened to me and my teenagers, with a Wet'suwet'en solidarity protest in downtown Peterborough. Instead of me taking them, they took me.

Watching my kiddos step up unprompted, and live their responsibilities as Michi Saagiig Nishnaabeg, was a beautiful relief.

I watched them as they used their bodies to build a beaver dam.

I watched them as they inherited both breathtaking beauty of Nishnaabewin and the struggle involved in birthing new worlds.

My beautiful relief sat beside another feeling well known to generations of Indigenous parents before me. The feeling of your chest closing in on laboured breath as you watch the beings you most love in the world, your little beans, step off the sidewalk and use their precious bodies—bodies that you've spent your life feeding, protecting, and stuffing vegetables into, to block the vehicles of white people, many of whom are visibly angry, some of whom make a regular practice of erasing and devaluing Indigenous minds, bodies, and spirits.

I thought of the parents of Colton Bushie, Tina Fontaine, and the family of one of my former students from Alexis Nakota Sioux First Nation, the brilliant Misty Potts, who was last seen in March of 2015.

This is not the world I wish to pass onto my children— a world where each year hope is further diminished.

There is currently a beaver resurgence of sorts happening on Turtle Island. Beavers have been seen round-dancing in malls, blockading ports and intersections, holding teach-ins at universities, handing out fully gnawed beaver sticks to hikers. Urban beavers have started to cut down trees in parks and along rivers build dams over urban creeks, flood the odd trail or basement. They've starred in their own Imax movie, enticed scientists into studies, and rejected the stereotype of felt hat for something truer to their form.

And while there are still those among us who would trap or shoot or relocate, there are also those that are watching quietly, learning, thinking through world making together with the beaver.

This final story is called Amikode, Beaver Heart.

Amikode

"OMG Parent, what is the point of building this friggen dam when we all know it's going to get destroyed by May and we will be right back to where we started."

Amikoons was making even the small things in life slightly more difficult for their parents and it was beginning to wear on Amik. There was a lot of actual work left to do which did not involve selfies, picking a song and listening to it for thirty-five seconds, and incessant complaining.

"Why are we building a dam anyway. This sucks. Let's build a selfie station."

The apocalypse could not come fast enough for Amik.

"Also, there is NO WAY I'm friggen going swimming."

Amik hoped, prayed, and worried that Amikoons was learning something today, but they weren't sure they were. Amikwag knowledge doesn't embed itself because of one's proximity.

Amik remembered the first time they were tasked with building a dam without their parents, and it was a moment.

It was one of the sharp edges of life.

A gathering of faith and hope.

An expulsion of uncertainty.

A feeling of betrayal at being left to do something on their own that eventually, with persistence, melted into a river of humility.

"The best parts of lonely."[36]

Amik remembered wishing they had paid more attention to the details. They wished they had been more engaged and that this process was less a series of steps and lists and more learned.

Here and now, Amik wondered what Amikoons would do in a similar situation. Would they even try to build the dam on their own? Or would they just sit there and drown in their abandonment, growing it until it festered into a series of tweets that would garnish heaps of likes and retweets reinforcing their own chosen uselessness and affirming the perceived injustice.

Amik felt like they were a hundred years old. The world had changed, without them. They felt cynical and out of touch and irrelevant, and they were.

Back in the day, before the genocide, Amikwag had a networked dam every hundred metres, and it was perfection. Amikwag's responsibilities were a foundational part of the circuitry and the life of stream. Dams managed water levels and flooding, removed excess nutrients and chemicals, worked as caring nurseries for salmonids and frogs, and made refuges for migrating songbirds. Before the zhaagansh got here, there were between 60 to 400 million of us and by the early 1900s that had dropped to 100,000.

Primarily because we are waterproof.

Amikoons wants to hear none of this, much less a parent lecture, so Amik lays off for now.

"Can you go cut some Aspens—about fifteen centimetres in diameter."

Amikoons leaves, headphones on, phone engaged, and Animkwag wonders how much longer than the required twenty minutes this will take.

Amikoons is back in one minute with no poplar.

"My teeth hurt and I couldn't find any."

Deep breaths.

"Let's go back together."

"Okay."

"Google 'How big is the biggest beaver dam.'"

"850m."

"WTH."

"WTH."

"Google 'Nictitating membrane.'"

"It's a third eyelid. Transparent. Functions like swim goggles. Do we have these?"

It was a constant battle to get the kid to gnaw on enough wood to keep their teeth a reasonable size and functional, and all kinds of treaties were made and broken trading gnawing for screen time. Amik's gut sank with the thought that Amikoons might not be able to cut down the poplar. There was also a kind of blind faith in this with the assumption that Amik was going to be skilled enough to get Amik's teeth into the bark in the first place.

This is all Amik's fault. They thought they were spending a reasonable amount of time on the land, more than most. Amik took gigs building selfie stations in the parks, bars, and airports, and mostly Amikoons stayed home with their screens. The stations consisted of a replicate lodge, small, but still enough for a family, some popular branches strategically placed, a couple of blue backdrops for sky and water, human foot prints and good lighting.

Yet here they were.

Spending a week on the creek building a dam they both knew would be destroyed by the city shortly after the photos and news stories.

Yet here they were.

Yet here they were, along with resentment, cynicism, self-doubt.

Yet here they were.

Amik wondered if their ancestors would even recognize them.

Amikoons wonders if they are going to learn anything that will improve their Minecraft beaver dam situation.

Amik selects two trees. Amikoons picks the song for chewing, asks Amik to start their tree and Amik obliges.

Amik takes a mouth wide open beside the gnaw marks selfie.

Amik says "race you."

Amik gnaws slowly, watching Amikoons progress out of the side of their eye. Amikoons is doing better than one might expect. It's working.

Amikoons is being an amikoons.

There is a swell of emotion in Amik, a mixture of relief, pride, and devastating sadness. A small victory that should never have been a victory in the first place.

Amik and their Amikoons carry the poplar back to the site in their mouths and place the branches on the shore.

Amikoons asks Amik for a pic of the carrying and Amik obliges because reciprocity isn't about giving back what you want, it is about giving back what is needed or what has been asked of you.

Amik eats some of the buds and branches while Amikoonse finds their gummy worms.

There is a moment.

A sort of sad, crappy moment, but a moment nonetheless.

Then Amikoons takes the branch in their mouth and swims towards the dam.

Nbwaakawin.

FINAL WORDS

I've shared four Nishnaabeg beaver stories with you. Four stories that embody the Nishnaabeg practice of Nbwaakawin.

The story of the Giant Beaver is one of imbalance, persistence, diplomacy, and generated consensus. Nanabush and beloved Nokomis work together to protect the land and water from Giant Beaver's dam, yet they don't destroy Giant Beaver. They find a way of working together and respecting each other's sovereignty so that both the world of the beaver and the Nishnaabeg world still breath.

"The Person Who Married a Beaver" reminds us that one can build and live in world predicated on consent.[37] It builds a world where the political economy of the Nishnaabeg and the beavers is founded upon consensus, sharing, and mutual respect. It reminds us we've always shared land and water, time and space with different nations. It reminds us that this practice of consent allows for different worlds to exist beside each other.

"AnabLog" demonstrates a different kind of intervention, one that amplifies and brings attention to destructive acts. It reminds us of the importance of kindness and caring and in the end demonstrates the use of oneself and one's gifts to propel more life.

The last story, "Amikode," is both a negation of colonialism and an affirmation of life-giving beaver practices and knowledge. Amikode is a messy resurgence. One begins with what they have. One does the best that they can.

We have some choices.

We can stand beside the pile of sticks blocking the flow of the river, and complain about inconveniences, or we can sit beside the pond and witness the beavers' life-giving brilliance.

Blockades are both a refusal and an affirmation.[38] An affirmation of a different political economy. A world built upon a different set of relationships and ethics. An affirmation of life.

That's why the words of Freda Huson, spokesperson of the Unist'ot'en camp, speak to the hearts of Indigenous Peoples all across Mikinaakong, when she says, "Our people's belief is that we are part of the land. The land is not separate from us. The land sustains us. And if we don't take care of her, she won't be able to sustain us, and we as a generation of people will die."[39]

That's why queer, trans, and Two Spirit artists and young people are, once again, on the frontlines leading solidarity occupations in Vancouver and Victoria, the prairies, and beyond.[40]

That's why Mohawk land protectors in Tyendinaga Mohawk Territory blocked the railway tracks.

That's why, a few short years ago, thousands organized and gathered at Standing Rock to block the Dakota Access Pipeline.[41]

This is why in 1995 the Ogoni Nine were executed for their refusal of Shell in Nigeria.[42]

This is why the Freedom School in Toronto made a tremendous "Black Kids Stand with Wet'suwet'en" banner in a joyful expression of solidarity.[43]

This isn't about pipelines, or jobs, or the best way to get our message out. This is about land and life for generations to come.

This is about the kind of worlds we collectively want to live it. Indigenous Worlds. Black Worlds. Beaver Worlds. Anti-Colonial Worlds.

We can have the same old arguments we've been having for centuries about inconvenience and the extra-legal nature of blockades.

We can pit jobs and the economy versus the environment.

We can perform superficial dances of reconciliation and dialogue and negotiate for the cheap gifts of economic and political inclusion.[44]

Or we can imagine other worlds.

We can remember the principled actions of the Dene nation in the 1970s opposing the Mackenzie Valley Pipeline, or the communities of Kanehsatà:ke and Kahnawake during the summer of 1990 and find ways to support families, clans, communities, and nations that stand up, and say no, you do not have our consent to build this golf course, pipeline, mine, hydro-dam, clear cut because we are very busy building a different world, and we are so deeply in love with our land, our cultures, our languages, and our families.

It is that love and care that Carrier Wit'at multidisciplinary artist and curator Whess Harman described emanating throughout the west coast Wet'suwet'en solidarity protest sites even in the face of state violence.[45]

Our current world is on fire, warming and melting at an unprecedented rate. The whole world should be standing behind the Wet'suwet'en hereditary chiefs and their clans, paying attention to the world they are refusing, observing how life behind the blockades renews a different vision, and witnessing the negation, the affirmation, and the generative refusal of blockades and those precious beaver dams.

Nbwaakawan.

Mii'iw

Miigwech

Kinanâskomitin

Hiy Hiy.

Notes

INTRODUCTION

1. Leanne Betasamosake Simpson, *Dancing On Our Turtle's Back: Stories of Nishnaabeg Re-Creation, Resurgence and a New Emergence* (Winnipeg: ARP Books, 2011), 54.

2. Simpson, *Dancing On Our Turtle's Back*, 55.

3. Richard Van Camp, Reviews of Leanne Betasamosake Simpson's *Islands of Decolonial Love*, ARP Books, accessed July 26, 2020, https://arpbooks.org/Books/I/Islands-of-Decolonial-Love.

4. Thomas King, Awards and Praise for Leanne Betasamosake's *This Accident of Being Lost*, House of Anansi Press, accessed July 26, 2020, https://houseofanansi.com/products/this-accident-of-being-lost.

5. Waubgeshig Rice, Reviews of Leanne Betasamosake Simpson's *Islands of Decolonial Love*, ARP Books, accessed July 26, 2020, https://arpbooks.org/Books/I/Islands-of-Decolonial-Love.

6. Katherena Vermette, Praise for Leanne Betasamosake Simpson and *This Accident of Being Lost,* House of Anansi, accessed July 26, 2020, https://houseofanansi.com/products/this-accident-of-being-lost.

A SHORT HISTORY OF THE BLOCKADE

1. For the translation of Nishnaabemowin words, please see the Ojibwe People's Dictionary, available online at https://ojibwe.lib.umn.edu.

2. Leanne Betasamosake Simpson, *As We Have Always Done: Indigenous Freedom through Radical Resistance* (Minneapolis: University of Minnesota Press, 2017), 23.

3. Simpson, *As We Have Always Done*, 23.

4. Leanne Betasamosake Simpson, "Being with the Land, Protects the Land," *Abolition Journal* (blog), February 21, 2020, https://abolitionjournal.org/being-with-the-land-protects-the-land-leanne-betasamosake-simpson/.

5. Kathryn Yusoff, *A Billion Black Anthropocenes or None* (Minneapolis: University of Minnesota Press, 2018), xiii.

6. M. NourbeSe Philip, "Jammin' Still," in *Bla_K: Essays and Interviews* (Toronto: BookThug, 2017), 13–37.

7. Glen Coulthard, "For Indigenous Nations to Live, Capitalism Must Die," *Unsettling American* (blog), March 13, 2020, https://unsettlingamerica.wordpress.com/2013/11/05/for-our-nations-to-live-capitalism-must-die/.

8. Coulthard, "For Indigenous Nations to Live."

9. Audra Simpson, *Mohawk Interruptus: Political Life across the Borders of Settler States* (Durham, NC: Duke University Press, 2014), 1–3.

10. Simpson, *Mohawk Interruptus*; Nick Estes, *Our History Is the Future: Standing Rock versus the Dakota Access Pipeline, and the Long Tradition of Indigenous Resistance* (New York: Verso Press, 2019), 248.

11. Estes, *Our History Is the Future*, 248.

12. The practice of wisdom.

13. Bill Mah, "Beavers Are Chewing Down an Unusual Number of River Valley Trees after Being Forced from Homes," *Edmonton Journal*, November 17, 2016, https://edmontonjournal.com/news/local-news/leave-it-to-beavers-dislodged-rodents-make-up-for-lost-time-by-chewing-down-more-river-valley-trees; Andrew McCutcheon, "Vancouver's Urban-Beaver Plan Focuses on Enhancing Habitats," *Globe and Mail*, February 6, 2016,

https://www.theglobeandmail.com/news/british-columbia/
vancouvers-urban-beaver-plan-focuses-on-enhancing-habitats/
article28530523/.

14. Edward Benton Banai, *The Mishomis Book: The Voice of the Ojibway*
    (St. Paul, MN: Indian Country Press, 1979).

15. Leanne Betasamosake Simpson, *Dancing on Our Turtle's Back:*
    Stories of Nishnaabeg Re-Creation, Resurgence and a New
    Emergence (Winnipeg: ARP Press, 2012), 124–27.

16. Simpson, *Dancing on Our Turtle's Back*, 124–27.

17. Simpson, *Dancing on Our Turtle's Back*, 124–27.

18. Simpson, *Dancing on Our Turtle's Back*, 124–27.

19. See Yellowknives Dene Knowledge Holder Fred Sangris's stories in
    "The Hero of the Dene," *UpHere Magazine*, n.d., accessed March
    13, 2020, https://uphere.ca/articles/hero-dene, and George
    Blondin, *Yamoria: The Lawmaker* (Edmonton: NewWest Press,
    1997).

20. Madeline Whetung, "(En)gendering Shoreline Law: Nishnaabeg
    Relational Politics along the Trent Severn Waterway," *Global*
    Environmental Politics 19, no. 3 (August 2019): 16–32,
    https://doi.org/10.1162/glep_a_00513.

21. Whetung, "(En)gendering Shoreline Law," 16.

22. Whetung, "(En)gendering Shoreline Law," 16.

23. Whetung, "(En)gendering Shoreline Law," 16.

24. "Nanabush and the Giant Beaver," by Sam Snake, Elijah
    Yellowhead, Alder York, and Annie King from the Chippewas of
    Rama, Mnjikaning First Nation; originally recorded and complied
    by Emerson and David Coatsworth in *The Adventures of Nanabush*
    (Toronto: Doubleday Canada, 1979), 17–23.

25. John Pinesi, "The Woman Who Married a Beaver," original
    transcription by William Jones, modern translation by Randy
    Valentine, in ed. Truman Michelson, and comp. William Jones,
    Ojibwa Texts, Publications of the American Ethnological Society,
    ed. Franz Boas (New York: E.J. Brill, 1919), vol. 7, pt. 1, xvi–xvii.

26. Heidi Kiiwetinepinesiik Stark, "Respect, Responsibility, and
    Renewal: The Foundations of Anishnaabe Treaty Making with the
    United States and Canada," *American Indian Culture and Research*
    Journal 34, no. 2 (2010): 145–64.

27. Stark, "Respect, Responsibility, and Renewal," 146.

28. Stark, "Respect, Responsibility, and Renewal," 157.

29. Stark, "Respect, Responsibility, and Renewal"; Whetung, "(En)gendering Shoreline Law."

30. Billy-Ray Belcourt, *NDN Coping Mechanisms: Notes from the Field* (Toronto: House of Anansi Press, 2019), 3.

31. Steve Daniels, *anaBlog*, accessed March 13, 2020, https://spinningtheweb.org/projects/anaBlog.html.

32. Jia Tolentino, *Trick Mirror: Reflections on Self-Delusion* (New York: Random House, 2019).

33. From "Poem 58" in *77 Fragments of a Familiar Ruin* by Thomas King (HarperCollins Publishers, 2019). Copyright © 2019 Thomas King. Used with permission of the author.

34. Leanne Betasamosake Simpson, lyrics from the song "Viscosity," from the forthcoming 2021 album *The Theory of Ice* (Toronto: You've Changed Records); also published in *Noopiming: The Cure for White Ladies* (Toronto: House of Anansi Press, 2020).

35. Willie Dunn, quoted in *60 Years of Indigenous Music Game Changers*, CBC Music, accessed March 13, 2020, https://www.cbc.ca/musicinteractives/gamechangers.

36. John K. Samson, from the lyrics to "Left and Leaving" on the album *Left and Leaving* (Winnipeg: G7 Welcoming Committee Records, 2000), lyrics published in *Lyrics and Poems 1997–2012* (Winnipeg: ARP Press, 2012), 40.

37. The original published version of this story is titled "The Woman Who Married a Beaver."

38. For a more comprehensive discussion of refusal, see Audra Simpson, *Mohawk Interruptus*.

39. Freda Huson, Unist'ot'en Hereditary Spokesperson, "Background of the Campaign," accessed March 13, 2020, https://unistoten.camp/no-pipelines/background-of-the-campaign/.

40. Lindsay Nixon, "Wet'suwet'en Strong," *Canadian Art* (blog), February 19, 2020, https://canadianart.ca/features/wetsuweten-strong/.

41. Estes, *Our History Is the Future*.

42. The Ogoni Nine were a group of nine activists from the Ogoni region of Nigeria who opposed the operating practices of the Royal

Dutch Shell oil corporation. Their members included writer and playwright Ken Saro-Wiwa, Saturday Dobee, Nordu Eawo, Daniel Gbooko, Paul Levera, Felix Nuate, Baribor Bera, Barinem Kiobel, and John Kpuine. They were executed in 1995 by the military dictatorship of General Sani Abacha. Also see Ruth Maclean, "Shell Awaits Court Ruling on Complicity in Deaths of Ogoni Nine," *The Guardian*, April 30, 2019, https://www.theguardian.com/world/2019/apr/30/shell-awaits-court-ruling-on-complicity-in-deaths-of-ogoni-nine.

43. Robyn Maynard, personal communication with the author, February 15, 2020.

44. Coulthard, "For Indigenous Nations to Live, Capitalism Must Die"; Glen Coulthard, *Red Skin, White Masks: Rejecting the Colonial Politics of Recognition* (Minneapolis: University of Minnesota Press, 2014).

45. Nixon, "Wet'suwet'en Strong."

CLC Kreisel Lecture Series

Published by University of Alberta Press and the Canadian Literature Centre / Centre de littérature canadienne

Printed in the USA
CPSIA information can be obtained
at www.ICGtesting.com
CBHW030357150724
11311CB00015B/52

9 781772 125382